# ANIMAL ANTICS

First published in 2009
Parragon
Queen Street House
4 Queen Street
Bath BA1 1HE, UK

Copyright © Parragon Books Ltd 2009

Designed, produced, and packaged by Stonecastle Graphics Ltd

Text by Daniel Gilpin
Designed by Sue Pressley and Paul Turner
Edited by Anthony John

ISBN 978-1-4075-7341-0

Printed in China

**Above:** *Emperor penguins, Antarctica.*
**Right:** *King penguin, Antarctica.*
**Previous page:** *Sifakas, Madagascar.*

# ANIMAL ANTICS

A photographic celebration of our funny friends

## Daniel Gilpin

Parragon

Bath・New York・Singapore・Hong Kong・Cologne・Delhi・Melbourne

Animals can be hilarious—they don't mean
to be, they just can't help it. More often than
not their funniest moments are missed, but here
they are caught on camera. Flick through this
book and see if you can stop yourself smiling.
Extended captions to the pictures are
collected at the back.

# Introduction

Animals often bring a smile to our faces. Many of their antics are things that we find amusing. They can even make us laugh out loud.

Of course, animals do not know when they are being funny. They are just doing what animals do. Young animals can be particularly entertaining to watch and photograph because often, like our own children, they just seem to want to play. Play is actually a very important part of growing up for many creatures. It allows them to practice the skills they will need to survive when they are older and it helps them learn where they stand in the natural order of things.

Animals play-fighting are actually testing their own strength and that of possible future rivals. A lion cub chasing its mother's tail may look amusing but for the lion cub it is deadly serious. The black tip of the tail represents imaginary prey, and following its movements and pouncing on it successfully hones the baby animal's ability to hunt. Also, for example, the

big cats are so similar to our domestic cats, but on a grander scale, that we can relate their behavior to that of our pets.

Young animals are also amusing because they often fall over. Just like human toddlers, they are much less steady on their legs than adults. Young creatures that climb, such as cats, are much more likely to lose their grip than their elders, but this is all part of their learning process. These moments, when animals show that they are fallible, come across as pure slapstick. We don't want them to get hurt—and usually they don't—but we cannot stop ourselves laughing. The instinct to laugh at such calamities is a very human one—most of us find it hard to suppress our mirth when another person falls over, as long as no harm is done.

The little accidents in animals' lives are one source of amusement to us but another is the apparent affection that they can show toward one another. We like the fact that animals might feel friendship and experience

*Above: Lions, Africa. **Opposite:** Gerenuks, Africa.*

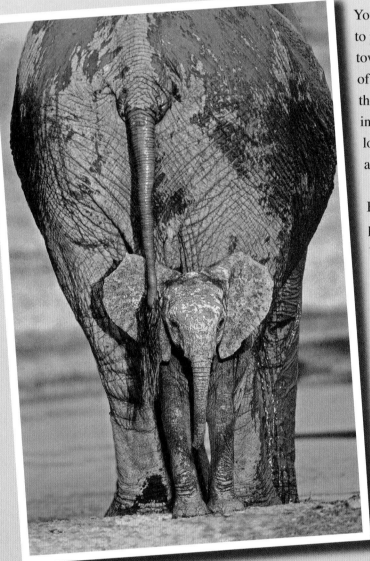

Young animals rely on their mothers for guidance and to protect them from danger, and mothers feel strongly toward their young because they represent the future of their genes. The same is true of human parents and their children, although many may not realize it. We instinctively feel incredible affection, which we call love, toward our children. Quite possibly, mother animals have similar feelings too.

Both young people and young animals mimic their parents—copying behavior is an important part of the learning process. When we see young animals mimicking their elders or trying to act in a grown-up way we feel the same way as we do when we see it in children. It's that cute thing again and we find it irresistible.

Animals amuse us for many reasons. Occasionally it is because of their strangeness, such as tree-climbing goats or deer stretching on their hind legs to reach that higher foliage, but often it is because they remind us of ourselves. While we might laugh at them, it is not out of cruelty, but rather with affection. Their antics brighten our days and make the world a better and sometimes funnier place to be. The elephant is a particularly social animal. These magnificent animals display great affection and family bonds and their protective attitude to their young is something we can all understand. A elephant calf scuttling for the shelter of its mother or holding its mother's tail is a delightful sight with which we can all empathize.

However, it is unrealistic always to credit animals with human reactions. For example, penguins can look very human with their upright stance and natural curiosity but the comparison can be taken too far.

Primates are animals of an order that includes apes, monkeys, and us. For this reason, we find apes and monkeys particularly intriguing and perhaps the easiest

emotions in a similar way to ourselves. Of course, we will never know exactly how animals feel about one another or if they actually feel affection in the same way as we do at all. That said, what looks like affection between some animals quite probably is. Group-living mammals in particular seem to crave bodily contact, whether it be grooming, nuzzling, or snuggling up together to sleep. In fact most mammals bond with one another at certain times in their lives, and so, for that matter, do birds, especially mothers with their young. When we see this behavior, it makes us smile because we recognize it. The word we might use to describe it is 'cute,' but just as with almost all animal behavior, it serves a purpose.

*Above: Elephants, Africa.*

to relate to. They have facial expressions that can be similar to our own, though the message conveyed should not always be interpreted as being the same as a human facial expression. Some animals seem to be naturally funny. Monkeys have natural mischievousness about them that makes them often seem like naughty children. Their inquisitiveness means that they get into everything. They steal food from one another and from behind people's backs. They almost seem to enjoy making a mess and knocking things over.

Monkeys are particularly funny because they don't just act like us, they look like us too. Some could almost be caricatures of people we know. Apes are even more like us in appearance. Orang-utans and chimps in particular have the ability to make us laugh, probably because they are considered the most intelligent animals on the planet after humans and therefore resemble us so much.

They themselves seem to laugh and enjoy human-like playful activities. Apes can also astonish us when they demonstrate their great intelligence with their tool-making skills and problem-solving ability.

Apes and monkeys are our closest relatives in the animal kingdom and their appearance mimics our own in many ways. Perhaps the most striking similarity between them and us is our faces, but other animals have faces that can make us smile too. Some creatures have faces that simply look odd—such as elephant seals, for example. Others that are more familiar can also look weird, however, especially when viewed from certain angles. The trick for the photographer is capturing the moments and the angles in which these creatures look amusing. To do this successfully requires a knowledge of the animals and how they are likely to behave, as well as a small amount of luck.

*Above: Lions, Africa.* 9

*Above and right:* Polar bears, Arctic Circle.

*Above and right:* Rhinoceroses, Africa.

*Above and left:* Chimpanzees, Africa.  *Following pages:* Orang-utans, Borneo.

*Above and right:* Giant Pandas, China.

***Above and right:*** *Meerkats, Africa.*

**Above and opposite:** *Tree frogs, Central America.*

*Above and opposite:* Tiger cubs, Asia.

**Above and opposite:** *Emperor penguins, Antarctica.*

**Top:** *Cheetahs, Africa.*

**Above:** *Kangaroos, Australia.*

***Opposite and above:*** *Hamadryas Baboons, North Africa.* **Top:** *Chacma Baboon, South Africa.* 33

*Above and right:* Giraffes, Africa.

*Above and right:* Lions, Africa.

**Top:** *Antarctic Fur Seal, Antarctic.* **Above:** *Gray Seal, Scotland.*

**Above:** *Leopard, Africa.*

*Top:* Puma cub, North America. ***Above:*** Leopard, Africa.

*Above and right: Hippopotamuses, Africa.*

Following pages: *Polar Bear, Arctic Circle.* 45

**Above:** *Elephants, Africa.*

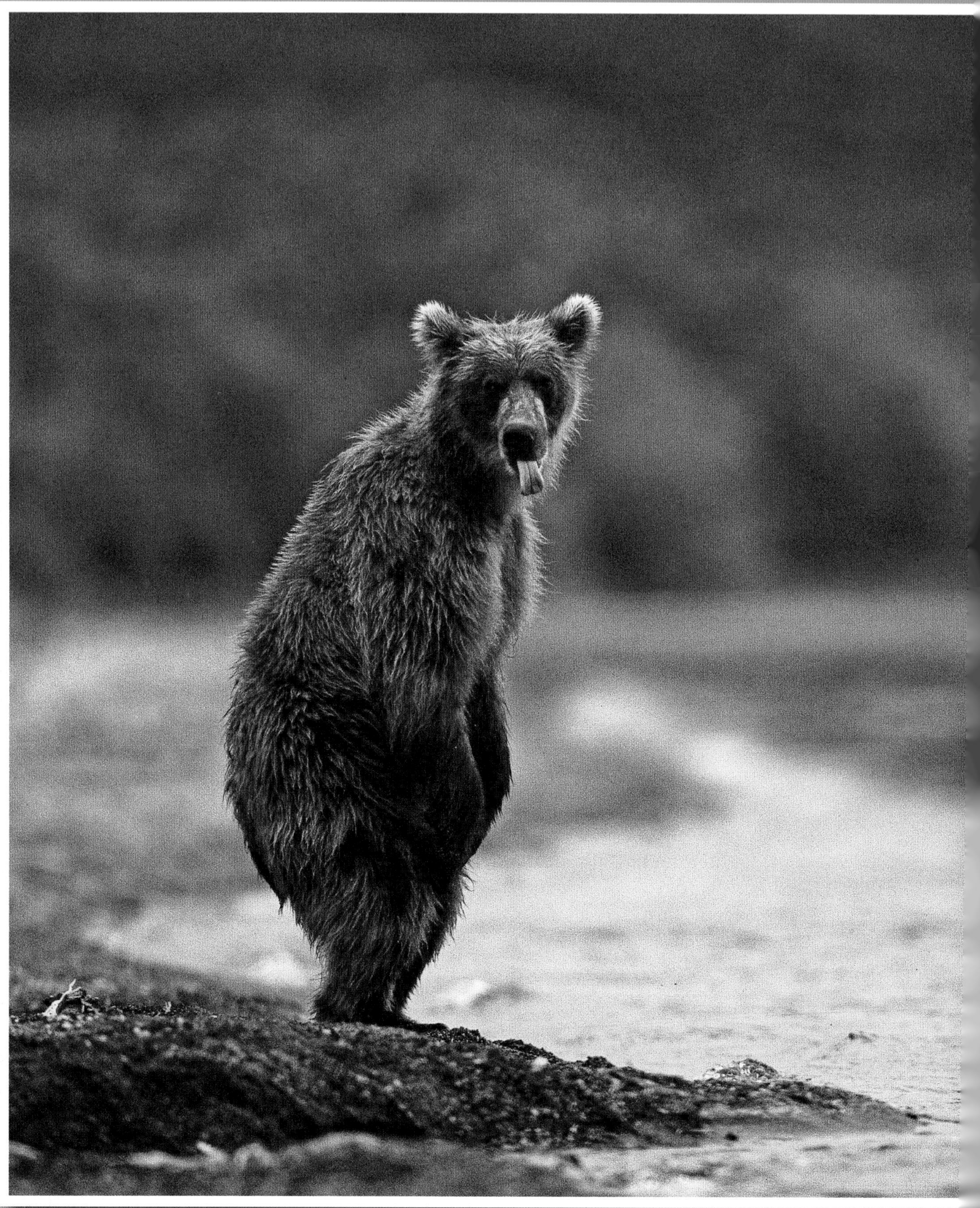

 ***Above and opposite:*** *Brown Bears, Canada.*

*Top:* Gray Squirrel, North America. *Above and opposite:* Chipmunks, North America.

*Above and Opposite:* Blue-footed Boobies, Galapagos Islands.

*Above and left: Meerkats, Africa.* 67

**Above:** *Labrador puppies, Europe.*

*Following pages:* *Baby Opossums, North America.* 69

**Above and right:** *Raccoon cubs, North America.*

# Animal Antics Photo Index

1
**Dancing Feet**
A female sifaka carries her youngster. Sifakas are lemurs from Madagascar and spend most of their time in the trees. When moving on the ground, they skip on their hind feet.

2
**Here's Looking At You, Kids**
Three emperor penguin chicks pose for the camera. Emperor penguins are the only birds to overwinter on Antarctica. The males huddle together, incubating the eggs on their feet.

3
**Watch the Birdie**
A king penguin examines a camera on a shingle beach. The king penguin is the world's largest penguin after the emperor, which it closely resembles.

4
**Balancing Act**
Goats clamber into a small tree in Africa to feed. Goats are extremely nimble animals and will go to great lengths to browse on leaves and other vegetation.

5
**Sun Loungers**
Meerkats live in some of Africa's hottest places. Like most animals around them, they relax during the middle of the day, being more active near to dawn and dusk.

6
**Big Yawn**
Few animals relax like lions. Sitting right at the top of the food chain, adult lions have no predators they need to look out for, so they can afford to lounge in peace.

7
**High Tea**
The gerenuk has evolved to browse on the low branches of trees. Unlike the giraffe, which can reach this food without stretching, this antelope has to stand on its back feet to feed.

8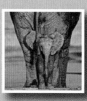
**Where's My Mum?**
Baby elephants always stay close to their mothers. Despite their size, they still need protection from large predators on the African plains.

9
**Big Brother**
Bonds within lion prides are strong. Females, which do most of the hunting, stay within the pride for life. Young males are driven out as soon as they become mature.

10A
**Snow Joke**
Polar bears can be surprisingly playful, especially when they are well fed. Seals make up the bulk of their diet, although carrion is also eaten when it can be found.

10B
**I Can't Bear It**
Even curled up like this, polar bears look big. In fact, they are the largest land predators on Earth. Reared up on its hind legs, a male polar bear can stand more than 10ft (3m) tall.

10C
**Just Chillin'**
This bear might look lazy, but polar bears are normally incredibly active animals. They spend most of their time on the move and sometimes wander for miles to find a meal.

11
**What's All That About?**
Polar bears like to know what is going on around them. The cubs are born during the winter in snow caves and emerge with their mothers the following spring.

12A
**Kiss Off**
This picture shows two black rhinoceroses. The black rhinoceros is a browsing animal rather than a grazer, and has a flexible top lip to help it pluck leaves from bushes.

**12B**

### Charge Of The Heavy Brigade

Rhinos have poor eyesight but very good senses of hearing and smell. As soon as they detect the sound or scent of possible danger, they charge toward it.

**13**

### Getting The Bird

A flock of oxpeckers gather on the backs of a rhinoceros and her calf. Oxpeckers feed on parasites such as ticks and so are tolerated by these massive herbivores.

**14**

### What Have I Done?

Chimpanzees are our closest relatives in the animal kingdom, sharing more than 95 percent of our DNA. As well as looking like us, they often act like us too.

**15A**

### Loose Lips

A chimpanzee's mouth is incredibly flexible. Like us, these apes eat a wide range of food, including various types of fruit, and meat when they can catch it.

**15B**

### Say Cheese!

The smile is a natural part of a chimp's facial repertoire. Unlike in humans, however, the smile is normally used to indicate anxiety or fear rather than happiness.

**15C**

### Not Listening

Like the rest of their bodies, chimpanzees' ears are very similar to our own. Young chimps, like this one, have pale skin, but this gradually grows darker with age.

**15D**

### This One's For You

Chimps have an incredible capacity to learn from those around them. This gesture, like the previous one, was learnt by the chimp's observation of humans.

**16**

### That Was A Hoot!

Orang-utans use sound to announce their presence to others. Orang-utan means 'man of the forest' in the Indonesian language. These three are adult males.

**18A**

### Strong-Arm Tactics

A young giant panda bends a bamboo stem. Giant pandas live in China and feed almost exclusively on bamboo, stripping off the leaves and side shoots.

**18B**

### Playing The Flute

It looks like it might be blowing, but this cub is actually chewing. Giant pandas have a pad on their front paws, which acts like a thumb, helping them to hold their food.

**19**

### High View

Giant pandas are surprisingly good climbers, despite their rotund appearance. Sadly, these animals are now very rare, with fewer than 2000 believed to remain in the wild.

**20A**

### Sitting Pretty

A meerkat relaxes in the sun. The meerkat is actually a species of mongoose and not much larger than a squirrel. Although this one is on his own, they are social animals.

**20B**

### Attennntion!

Meerkats stand up to scan the area around them. Although they are carnivores, they have many predators themselves and are always on the lookout for danger.

**21**

### Standing Out

Meerkats live in groups known as mobs, gangs, or clans. When standing on their hind legs like this, they use their tails to help prop themselves up.

**22**

### Sticky Fingers

As their name suggests, tree frogs spend most of their time off the ground. They have adhesive pads on their toes that enable them to grip leaves and branches.

**23**

### Slippery Skin

Like all frogs, tree frogs are amphibians and have porous skin that loses water. As a consequence, they prefer humid habitats and are most active after rain.

24A

### Sleeping Like A Log
This tiny tiger cub has nodded off in the sun. Like domestic kittens, tiger cubs spend a lot of their time asleep, giving their little bodies time to rest as they grow.

24B

### Top And Tail
Tigers are born with their eyes closed and these cubs have not had theirs open for long. Female tigers usually have three or four cubs in a litter.

25

### Paws For A Snooze
Like most baby animals, tiger cubs seem to have disproportionately big feet. As with adults, their claws are normally sheathed but can be pushed out when needed.

26A

### Walk This Way
Four emperor penguin chicks follow an adult. Emperor penguin chicks beg their parents for food, which takes the form of regurgitated fish and squid, brought back from the sea.

26B

### Slip Sliding Away
Emperor penguin chicks form crèches while their parents are at sea. Sticking together gives them some protection from predators and a chance to get to know their peers.

27A

### Dancing On Ice
Emperor penguins only lay a single egg and raise one chick a year. These two were photographed at the edge of a crèche while their parents were absent.

27B

### Look At It My Way...
Emperor penguin chicks are covered with thick fluffy down, which keeps them warm in the Antarctic weather. As they grow up, this down is shed for more waterproof feathers.

28

### Right There—That's It!
A young cheetah playfully scratches at his mother's ear. Cheetah cubs stay with their mother until they are about 18 months old, when they are finally able to hunt alone.

29

### Give Us A Cuddle
Lion cubs love a bit of rough and tumble, but like all baby animals they also spend a lot of their time resting or asleep. Snuggling up like this helps strengthen sibling bonds.

30

### Seconds Out, Round One
Kangaroos are famous boxers. Males size each other up like this before fighting to establish dominance and the right to mate with females.

32

### Take It Easy
A hamadryas baboon relaxes in a tree. The ancient Egyptians kept these intelligent baboons as household pets, much as we keep dogs today.

33A

### So That's What My Tail Looks Like
A young chacma baboon attempts the monkey equivalent of a headstand. The chacma is one of the most common species of baboon, found throughout much of southern Africa.

33B

### Three Wise Monkeys
See no evil, hear no evil, speak no evil. These three hamadryas baboons are all females. The males of this species are bigger and have much larger manes.

34A

### Who Are You Looking At?
A baby giraffe does his best to look tough. Female giraffes give birth standing up, so this youngster entered the world with a thud, falling the best part of 7ft (2m) to the floor.

34B

### High Jump
Like most plant-eating mammals, giraffes are quick to find their feet after birth. Before they are able to run, they are very vulnerable to attacks from predators.

35

### Give Us A Kiss
Lifting up his top lip, this baby giraffe sticks out his tongue. Once he has grown up, his tongue will be much longer and used for stripping leaves from twigs.

**Hold Tight, Please**

A lion cub pulls at his mother's tail while an older sibling follows a little way behind. Lion cubs often play with adults' tails in this way, enjoying the physical contact.

**Lion Line Up**

Four cubs obediently follow their mother. Lionesses give birth on their own in cover and lead their young to the pride when they are a few weeks old.

**One-Sided View**

Lionesses are extremely tolerant of their cubs. The youngsters learn how to hunt by watching their elders, but this one is perhaps a bit closer than it needs to be!

**Wait For Me!**

A lion cub grabs hold of his mother's tail. Lion cubs are born with spots, but these gradually fade. The spots on this cub's legs are still clearly visible.

**Look At It This Way**

A young Antarctic fur seal looks into the camera. This pup will shed its pale coat as it grows older to take on a more adult pelt of dark brown.

**Too Funny For Words**

This humorous pose was caught as this gray seal yawned. Gray seals haul out on to sandbanks like this, both to rest after feeding and to breed.

**Scratch With Mother**

Sitting in the sun can be hot and itchy, and these Galapagos sea lions live right on the equator. They share their island home with giant tortoises and penguins.

**Having A Laugh**

Three plains zebras show the photographer their teeth. Of the three species of zebra the plains zebra is the most common, occurring across much of southern and eastern Africa.

**Mouthy In The Middle**

Like their domesticated relatives, horses and donkeys, zebras are quite vocal animals. They call both in alarm and to announce their presence to potential rivals or mates.

**Two Heads Are Better Than One**

Zebras' stripes help their bodies merge together, as this picture clearly shows. This makes it harder for predators to target individuals in herds.

**Cosy Spot**

A leopard lounges lazily up on a branch. Like many species of cats, leopards are largely nocturnal and spend the daylight hours resting or asleep.

**Get A Grip**

A puma cub clambers precariously high in the remains of a dead tree. Like lion cubs, puma cubs are spotty to help camouflage them from potential predators.

**Branching Out**

This leopard looks like it could be a little more comfy. Leopards not only sleep in trees, they also drag their kills up into them to protect them from lions.

**Odd Couple**

This young hippopotamus has made an unusual friend—a giant tortoise that shares his enclosure. In the wild, hippos are naturally social animals that seek out company.

**Gentle Persuasion**

This tiny hippo has only just been born and needs a little help to get to his feet. Despite seeming clumsy, female hippos make attentive mothers, taking good care of their young.

**Open Wide**

Despite their large canines and huge mouths, hippos are herbivores. In the wild they spend their days in water and come out on to land to graze at night.

**Bear Behind**

A polar bear shows the undersides of its paws as it prepares to slide down an icy slope. Polar bears have very large paws to spread their weight and help prevent them sinking into snow.

**Big Babies**

The African elephant is the world's largest land animal. At birth it weighs more than a full-grown man and adult males can tip the scales at over 7 tons.

**Bit Of A Stretch**

A red squirrel shows its agility as it nibbles on a nut. Red squirrels are Britain's only native squirrels; the more common gray squirrel was introduced from North America.

**Holding It Together**

A female reed bunting hangs acrobatically in a reed bed. Reed buntings are widespread across both Europe and Asia, and also occur in western North America.

**Tough Customer**

Elephant seals could hardly be better named. They have thick, gray-brown skin and are massive animals, weighing up to 3 tons. The males even have a small trunk.

**My Lips Are Sealed**

A baby orang-utan puts on his best innocent look. Orang-utans live almost entirely on a diet of fruit, which they find in the trees of their rainforest home.

**Standing Out**

A brown bear rears up on its hind legs. Bears do this for two main reasons: to appear more threatening to rivals or to get a better look at distant objects.

**Look, Mum, Look!**

Baby bears follow their mother everywhere. North America's brown bears are known as grizzlies because of the often pale and grizzled appearance of their fur.

**See, I Can Touch My Toes**

Brown bears are big but they can still be acrobatic. The brown bear is the world's largest land carnivore after the polar bear, weighing up to three-quarters of a ton.

**Hands Up Who Likes Honey**

The large, flat pads on the feet of a brown bear help to support the great weight of its body. Each of the feet, or paws, is also armed with five long, thick claws.

**The Big Sleep**

Male lions are larger than females and have a thick mane of hair. This makes them look even bigger than they are and offers some protection to the neck during fights.

**Top Of The Heap**

A gray squirrel sits on top of his pile of nuts. Squirrels gather nuts in the fall and then bury them in the soil to be dug up later, when food is scarce.

**Cheeky!**

A chipmunk takes supplies back to its burrow. These little rodents have cheek pouches that expand, allowing them to carry much more food than they could swallow.

**Bit Of A Mouthful**

Like squirrels, chipmunks gather food when it is plentiful to last them through the winter. Peanuts put out by friendly humans are a favorite treat.

**I Hate Eating Greens**

A wolf cub chews on a blade of grass. Like domestic dogs, wolves eat grass and other plant material for the fiber, which helps with their digestion.

**What's That Smell?**

A young lion yawns and inadvertently makes a funny face in the process. Like all cats, lions have a good sense of smell but they rely more on their vision and hearing to hunt.

# PICTURE INDEX

## PICTURE CREDITS

*a = above, b = below, c = center, r = right, l = left, bg = background*